780

A ROOKIE BIOGRAPHY

LEONARD BERNSTEIN

All-American Musician

By Marlene Toby

Children's Press ®

A Division of Grolier Publishing
New York   London   Hong Kong   Sydney
Danbury, Connecticut

Leonard Bernstein 1918-1990

Library of Congress Cataloging-in-Publication Data

Toby, Marlene.
    Leonard Bernstein: all-American musician / by Marlene Toby.
        p. cm. — (A Rookie biography)
    Summary: Examines the life and career of the famous composer, conductor,
pianist, and teacher.
    Includes index.
    ISBN 0-516-04273-4
    1. Bernstein, Leonard, 1918-1990—Juvenile literature 2. Musicians—United States—
Biography—Juvenile literature. [1. Bernstein, Leonard, 1918-1990. 2. Musicians.]
I. Title. II. Series: Toby, Marlene. Rookie biography.
ML3830.B48G73 1995
780' 092 — dc20
[B]   95-19070
                                                CIP
                                                AC

Leonard Bernstein lived from
1918 to 1990. He was a pianist,
a conductor, a composer, and
a teacher. This is his story.

CONTENTS

Chapter 1

Something Good

Lenny Bernstein was
small and often sick.
He had asthma. Colds
kept him out of school.

But Lenny was very bright
and wanted to know how
and why things happen.
He filled his days with
many adventures and
discoveries.

One Saturday morning,
Lenny's father took him
and his sister Shirley to
the Jewish temple. That
day changed Lenny's life.

At the temple, Lenny
heard singing and music.
He didn't want the organ
to stop playing. It was
the most beautiful sound
he had ever heard!

A *Jewish temple in New York City at the
turn of the century*

Some time later, Lenny's
Aunt Clara moved her piano
to the Bernstein home.
It was old and ugly.
But Lenny fell in love
with that piano at once.

He would think of melodies
and then make up music to
go with them. Hour after
hour he played.

"Do your homework!"
said his parents. But
Lenny kept playing.

"Go to bed!" said his
parents. But Lenny
kept playing.

He could not stop. He
had found something that
made him very happy. He
did not want anything to
take that away from him.

Chapter 2

Big Changes

Lenny asked his father if
he could take piano lessons.
"No," said his father. But
Lenny was stubborn. He
kept asking. After a while,
his father said yes.

Later, Lenny's father found
the right piano teacher for
him. Her name was Helen
Coates. She knew Lenny
was special. She taught
him about all kinds of music.

Before long, Lenny was
a different boy. In school
his grades got better, and
he did well in sports. He
made many friends.

Music had given Lenny
a whole new look on
life. It was magic.

Lenny's father was happy
to see the change in him.
But he didn't want Lenny
to make music his career.
He didn't think a person
could make a good living
playing music.

Memorial Hall at Harvard University in 1935

In 1935, Lenny went to
study music at Harvard
University in Massachusetts.

Leonard Bernstein (third from left) graduated from the Curtis Institute of Music in 1941. Dr. Randall Thompson (seated) was director of the Institute from 1939 to 1941.

When he graduated, he went to the Curtis Institute of Music in Philadelphia to study conducting.

Conducting is one of the
hardest jobs in music.
Lenny said that a conductor
has to play the whole
orchestra the way other
people play only one
instrument. He said
a conductor "must make
the orchestra love music
as he loves it."

Lenny thought he
could do it. So did
some important people
in the world of music.

During the summer, Lenny
studied conducting with
Serge Koussevitzky
(koo suh viht skee),
the great conductor of the
Boston Symphony Orchestra.

Koussevitzky liked Lenny
and became his friend.
After Lenny finished school,
the two men kept in touch.

For a while it seemed as
though Lenny would never
find a good job in music.
Sometimes he thought that
his father had been right
about a music career.

Serge Koussevitzky (left) and Artur Rodzinski (right)

Then on Lenny's 25th birthday,
Koussevitzky helped him meet
Artur Rodzinski, conductor
of the New York Philharmonic.
Rodzinski asked Lenny to be
his assistant.

What a birthday present!
Lenny wouldn't conduct real
performances, but he would
work with the orchestra.
That was enough for him.

Chapter 3

The Young Conductor

Young Leonard Bernstein had
been writing his own music
for a long time. On November
13, 1943, one of his pieces
was performed at Town Hall
in New York City.

The performance went well.
Bernstein stayed up late and
celebrated at a party with
his friends.

Opposite page: Leonard Bernstein in 1945

The next morning, his phone rang. He was told that the guest conductor for that day had the flu. Rodzinski couldn't get to New York City through the snow, so Bernstein would have to conduct the New York Philharmonic's performance that afternoon.

Opposite page: As conductor, Bernstein used hand signals and facial expressions to tell musicians how to play the music.

21

Bernstein had never
practiced that piece of
music with the orchestra.
So he studied it — hard
and fast. Then, at three
o'clock, he walked onto the
stage and began conducting.

*Hand signals can ask certain musicians to
play softly or loudly, or with more feeling.*

Leonard Bernstein was great.
The audience roared. The
newspapers raved. Soon the
music world knew about young
Leonard Bernstein.

The next year he conducted
almost ninety concerts
throughout the United States.
Sometimes he played the
piano and conducted at the
same time.

Here, Leonard Bernstein directs an orchestra by keeping time with his hands. Conductors also use batons.

In 1948, Leonard Bernstein got a big welcome from the people of Beersheba, Israel. Here he conducted the Israel Philharmonic Orchestra.

World War II ended
in 1945. A year later,
Bernstein conducted
in Europe. Then he
went to Israel.

The concerts in Israel meant
a great deal to him. He was
Jewish. He knew how his
people had suffered during
World War II.

*At Beersheba, Leonard Bernstein conducted
and also played the piano.*

Leonard Bernstein, traveling with his sister Shirley

Soon Bernstein's life was
so full and busy that he
needed help. So Helen
Coates — once his teacher —
came to work for him.

Helen did all the things he
had no time for. That left
Bernstein free to make
all the music he could.
And he did.

Chapter 4

All Kinds of Music

Leonard Bernstein liked
many kinds of music, and
he wrote many kinds, too.

One of his major pieces was
called the *Jeremiah Symphony*.
He used Jewish melodies in it
and words from the Bible.

When he was 21 years old,
he wrote a set of funny
songs for kids called
I Hate Music.

Leonard Bernstein had to practice long hours with orchestras.

On The Town *was created by Betty Comden, Adolph Green, Leonard Bernstein, and Jerome Robbins. Later, it was made into a movie (opposite page).*

Then he wrote a ballet score about three young sailors. *Fancy Free* did so well that Bernstein asked his friends Adolph Green and Betty Comden to help him turn it into a musical. The musical, *On the Town*, opened in 1944.

Bernstein's music was fresh. It sounded very American. But some people thought that Bernstein should not write music.

"Be more serious about
your work," they said.
"Forget about writing music.
Just conduct." But Bernstein
said that "the only way one
can really say anything about
music is to write music."

Bernstein couldn't just conduct.
He was so full of music —
all sorts of wonderful music.
He just had to let it all out.

Leonard Bernstein shows his daughter Jamie some tricks of the trade. Below, he poses with his wife Felicia, daughter Jamie, and son Alexander Serge.

In 1951, Bernstein married Felicia Cohn, an actress from Chile. She played the piano and loved music, too. Eventually, they had two girls and a boy.

In 1957, Bernstein's most
famous musical,
West Side Story, was
performed. It is a love
story like Romeo and
Juliet. But it is set
in modern times in New
York City.

West Side Story was a big
hit. It even became a movie.
Some of the favorite songs
from that musical are
"I Feel Pretty," "There's
a Place for Us," "Tonight,"
and "Maria."

Dancers perform on the movie set of West Side Story.

Chapter 5

So Much to Do

In 1958, Bernstein became
musical director of the
New York Philharmonic.
He still loved conducting,
but kept writing music, too.

He wanted to teach people
about music. He wanted
children to know its magic.
So he did a television series
called *Young People's Concerts*.
It was a big success.

Mr. and Mrs. Bernstein show their son Lenny how they feel about his first concert in 1958.

Bernstein accepts a medal from the Kennedys for his performance at the Kennedy Center in 1971.

In 1971, Bernstein wrote the music for a Catholic Mass to celebrate the opening of the Kennedy Center for the Performing Arts in Washington, D.C. Many people praised his work.

Five years later, he and
his wife Felicia separated.
Two years later, she died.
Bernstein was sad but stayed
busy. That was the best thing.

Leonard and his wife Felicia in 1977

The Berlin Wall in Germany, February 20, 1990

In 1989, Bernstein conducted
a very special concert in East
Berlin, Germany. Musicians
came from all over the world
to play in this concert.

They were celebrating freedom
and the fall of the Berlin Wall
that had divided Germany for
so many years.

The piece Bernstein conducted was Beethoven's *Ninth Symphony*. A choir sang the last part of the symphony. It is a hymn called "Ode to Joy." But the singers changed the word "joy" to "freedom" when they sang it. Bernstein told them, "I am sure we have Beethoven's blessing."

In Berlin, Bernstein conducted an orchestra and choir made up of people from both East and West Germany.

On October 14, 1990,
Leonard Bernstein had
a heart attack and died.
He was 72 years old.
He had lived a full life.
However, there were still
so many things he had
wanted to do.

One musician said that
"Lenny led four lives." All
of them were full of what
he loved most — music.

Leonard Bernstein conducted in New York for the last time on March 7, 1990.

Important Dates

1918   August 25 — Born in Lawrence, Massachusetts, to Jennie and Sam Bernstein

1928   Began piano lessons

1935   Began studies at Harvard University, Cambridge, Massachusetts

1939   Began studies at the Curtis Institute of Music, Philadelphia, Pennsylvania

1943   Became assistant conductor of the New York Philharmonic; conducted his first performance of Philharmonic

1946   First conducted in Europe

1948   First conducted in Israel

1951   Married Felicia Montealegre Cohn

1957   *West Side Story* first performed

1958   Became musical director of the New York Philharmonic

1971   Composed *Mass* for opening of Kennedy Center, Washington, D.C.

1989   Conducted in East Berlin to celebrate fall of Berlin Wall

1990   October 14 — Died of heart failure

Index

Page numbers in boldface type indicate illustrations.

PHOTO CREDITS